C000008971

DON'T PANIC

· · · · · · · · · · · · · · · ·
YOU'RE ONLY
· · · · · · · · · · · · · · · ·

30!

summersdale

DON'T PANIC, YOU'RE ONLY 30!

This revised edition copyright © Summersdale Publishers Ltd, 2018
First published in 2011 as *Keep Calm You're Only 30*

Compiled by Vicky Edwards

An Hachette UK Company
www.hachette.co.uk

Summersdale Publishers Ltd
Part of Octopus Publishing Group Limited
Carmelite House
50 Victoria Embankment
LONDON
EC4Y 0DZ

www.summersdale.com

Printed and bound in the Czech Republic

ISBN: 978-1-78685-292-2

Substantial discounts on bulk quantities of Summersdale books
are available to corporations, professional associations and other
organisations. For details contact general enquiries: telephone:
+44 (0) 1243 771107 or email: enquiries@summersdale.com.

TO..Sharon......

FROM..Mam..........
18/09/2018.

CONTENTS

ANOTHER YEAR

OLDER

—

AGE IS JUST
A NUMBER. IT'S
TOTALLY IRRELEVANT
UNLESS, OF COURSE,
YOU HAPPEN TO BE
A BOTTLE OF WINE.

—

JOAN COLLINS

THIRTY WAS SO STRANGE
FOR ME. I'VE REALLY
HAD TO COME TO TERMS
WITH THE FACT THAT
I AM NOW A WALKING
AND TALKING ADULT.

C. S. LEWIS

THIRTY?
FLIRTY
AND
DIRTY!

ANONYMOUS

TIME AND TIDE WAIT
FOR NO MAN, BUT TIME
ALWAYS STANDS STILL
FOR A WOMAN OF 30.

Robert Frost

THE WAY I SEE IT, YOU SHOULD LIVE EVERY DAY LIKE IT'S YOUR BIRTHDAY.

Paris Hilton

THERE WAS A
STAR DANCED,

AND UNDER THAT WAS I BORN.

William Shakespeare

WHEN YOU TURN 30, A WHOLE NEW THING HAPPENS: YOU SEE YOURSELF ACTING LIKE YOUR PARENTS.

Blair Sabol

THIRTY-FIVE IS
A VERY ATTRACTIVE
AGE; LONDON SOCIETY
IS FULL OF WOMEN
WHO HAVE OF THEIR
OWN FREE CHOICE
REMAINED 35
FOR YEARS.

Oscar Wilde

FEW WOMEN
ADMIT THEIR AGE.
FEW MEN ACT THEIRS.

ANONYMOUS

WHEN THEY
TELL ME I'M
TOO OLD TO
DO SOMETHING,
I ATTEMPT IT
IMMEDIATELY.

Pablo Picasso

MEN ARE LIKE WINE. SOME TURN TO VINEGAR,

BUT THE BEST IMPROVE WITH AGE.

C. E. M. Joad

—

EVENTUALLY YOU WILL
REACH A POINT WHEN
YOU STOP LYING ABOUT
YOUR AGE AND START
BRAGGING ABOUT IT.

—

WILL ROGERS

YOU'RE NOT
AGEING
...
YOU'RE
MARINATING.

ANONYMOUS

THE BEST BIRTHDAYS OF
ALL ARE THOSE THAT
HAVEN'T ARRIVED YET.

Robert Orben

**ALL THE WORLD
IS A BIRTHDAY CAKE,
SO TAKE A PIECE,
BUT NOT TOO MUCH.**

George Harrison

A BIRTHDAY IS JUST
THE FIRST DAY OF
ANOTHER 365-DAY
JOURNEY AROUND
THE SUN.

ENJOY THE TRIP.

Anonymous

NO WOMAN SHOULD EVER BE QUITE ACCURATE ABOUT HER AGE. IT LOOKS SO CALCULATING.

Oscar Wilde

EVERY YEAR ON
YOUR BIRTHDAY,
YOU GET A CHANCE
TO START NEW.

Sammy Hagar

JUST WHAT I ALWAYS WANTED

WE KNOW WE'RE GETTING
OLD WHEN THE ONLY
THING WE WANT FOR
OUR BIRTHDAY IS NOT
TO BE REMINDED OF IT.

ANONYMOUS

WHY IS BIRTHDAY
CAKE THE ONLY
FOOD YOU CAN
BLOW ON AND
SPIT ON AND
EVERYBODY RUSHES
TO GET A PIECE?

Bobby Kelton

—

A GIFT CONSISTS NOT
IN WHAT IS DONE OR
GIVEN, BUT IN THE
INTENTION OF THE
GIVER OR DOER.

—

SENECA

A TRUE FRIEND
REMEMBERS
YOUR BIRTHDAY,

**BUT NOT
YOUR AGE.**

Anonymous

A GIFT,
WITH A KIND
COUNTENANCE,
IS A
DOUBLE
PRESENT.

Thomas Fuller

GOD GAVE US THE GIFT
OF LIFE; IT IS UP TO US
TO GIVE OURSELVES
THE GIFT OF LIVING WELL.

Voltaire

I THINK, AT A CHILD'S
BIRTH, IF A MOTHER COULD
ASK A FAIRY GODMOTHER TO
ENDOW IT WITH THE MOST
USEFUL GIFT, THAT GIFT
SHOULD BE CURIOSITY.

Eleanor Roosevelt

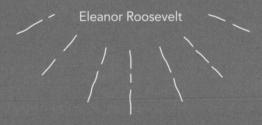

**A HUG
IS THE PERFECT GIFT;
ONE SIZE FITS ALL,
AND NOBODY MINDS
IF YOU EXCHANGE IT.**

Anonymous

YOUTH IS
THE GIFT OF NATURE,

BUT AGE IS
A WORK OF ART.

Garson Kanin

THERE ARE 364 DAYS
WHEN YOU MIGHT
GET UN-BIRTHDAY
PRESENTS... AND ONLY
ONE FOR BIRTHDAY
PRESENTS, YOU KNOW.

LEWIS CARROLL

BIRTHDAYS ARE NATURE'S WAY OF TELLING US TO EAT MORE CAKE.

ANONYMOUS

—

BIRTHDAYS ARE GOOD FOR YOU. STATISTICS SHOW THAT THE PEOPLE WHO HAVE THE MOST LIVE THE LONGEST.

—

LARRY LORENZONI

**THE BEST WAY TO
REMEMBER YOUR
WIFE'S BIRTHDAY IS
TO FORGET IT ONCE.**

E. Joseph Cossman

GRIN AND BEAR IT

GETTING OLD IS A
FASCINATING THING.
THE OLDER YOU GET,
**THE OLDER YOU
WANT TO GET.**

Keith Richards

A WOMAN NEVER FORGETS HER AGE

– ONCE SHE HAS DECIDED WHAT IT IS.

Stanley Davis

—

I'M KIND OF COMFORTABLE WITH GETTING OLDER BECAUSE IT'S BETTER THAN THE OTHER OPTION, WHICH IS BEING DEAD. SO I'LL TAKE GETTING OLDER.

—

GEORGE CLOONEY

IF YOU CARRY
YOUR CHILDHOOD
WITH YOU, YOU NEVER
BECOME OLDER.

Tom Stoppard

THERE IS AN ANTI-AGEING POSSIBILITY, BUT IT HAS TO COME FROM WITHIN.

Susan Anton

I THINK ALL THIS TALK
ABOUT AGE IS FOOLISH.
EVERY TIME I'M
ONE YEAR OLDER,
EVERYONE ELSE IS TOO.

Gloria Swanson

AGE IS AN ISSUE OF MIND OVER MATTER.

IF YOU DON'T MIND, IT DOESN'T MATTER.

Anonymous

YOU ARE NEVER TOO OLD TO SET ANOTHER GOAL OR TO DREAM A NEW DREAM.

Les Brown

NO ONE
CAN AVOID AGEING,
BUT AGEING
PRODUCTIVELY
IS SOMETHING ELSE.

Katharine Graham

THE ONLY TIME YOU
REALLY LIVE FULLY IS
FROM 30 TO 60. THE
YOUNG ARE SLAVES
TO DREAMS; THE OLD
SERVANTS OF REGRETS.
ONLY THE MIDDLE-AGED
HAVE ALL THEIR FIVE
SENSES IN THE KEEPING
OF THEIR WITS.

HERVEY ALLEN

AGE IS A NUMBER AND MINE IS UNLISTED.

ANONYMOUS

WHEN IT COMES TO AGE WE'RE ALL IN THE SAME BOAT,

ONLY SOME OF US HAVE BEEN ABOARD A LITTLE LONGER.

Leo Probst

DO A LITTLE DANCE, MAKE A LITTLE LOVE

—

YOU KNOW YOU'RE
GETTING OLD WHEN
YOUR IDEA OF HOT,
FLAMING DESIRE IS
A BARBECUED STEAK.

—

VICTORIA FABIANO

NO ONE GROWS OLD BY LIVING – ONLY BY LOSING INTEREST IN LIVING.

Marie Ray

IF WRINKLES MUST BE
WRITTEN UPON OUR
BROWS, LET THEM NOT BE
WRITTEN UPON THE HEART.
**THE SPIRIT SHOULD
NEVER GROW OLD.**

James A. Garfield

THE MORE YOU PRAISE AND CELEBRATE YOUR LIFE,

THE MORE
THERE IS IN LIFE
TO CELEBRATE.

Oprah Winfrey

**LIVE YOUR LIFE
AND FORGET
YOUR AGE.**

Norman Vincent Peale

**DO I EXERCISE?
WELL I ONCE JOGGED
TO THE ASHTRAY.**

Will Self

SEX IN YOUR TWENTIES? 'YES, YES, YES – AGAIN.'

SEX IN YOUR THIRTIES? 'OW, MY HIP.'

Caroline Rhea

LET US CELEBRATE THE OCCASION WITH WINE AND SWEET WORDS.

Titus Maccius Plautus

**EARLY TO RISE AND
EARLY TO BED MAKES
A MAN HEALTHY,
WEALTHY AND DEAD.**

JAMES THURBER

IT'S
IMPORTANT
TO HAVE A
TWINKLE IN
YOUR WRINKLE.

Anonymous

—

HE HAS A PROFOUND RESPECT FOR OLD AGE. ESPECIALLY WHEN IT'S BOTTLED.

—

GENE FOWLER

YOU KNOW YOU'RE
GETTING OLD WHEN
THE FIRST THING YOU
DO AFTER YOU'RE
DONE EATING

IS LOOK FOR A PLACE
TO LIE DOWN.

Louie Anderson

I CAN STILL ROCK LIKE
A SON OF A B*TCH.

Ozzy Osbourne

YOUNG AT HEART

I CAN STILL CUT THE MUSTARD...

I JUST NEED HELP OPENING THE JAR!

Anonymous

IF YOU OBEY

ALL THE RULES,

YOU MISS

ALL THE FUN.

KATHARINE HEPBURN

BASHFULNESS IS AN
ORNAMENT TO YOUTH,
**BUT A REPROACH
TO OLD AGE.**

Aristotle

YOU KNOW YOU'RE
GROWING OLD
WHEN THE LIGHT
OF YOUR LIFE

IS THE ONE
IN THE FRIDGE.

Hal Roach

ANYONE WHO
STOPS LEARNING IS OLD,
WHETHER AT 20 OR 80.
ANYONE WHO KEEPS
LEARNING STAYS YOUNG.
THE GREATEST THING IN
LIFE IS TO KEEP YOUR
MIND YOUNG.

Henry Ford

I'M HAPPY TO
REPORT THAT MY
INNER CHILD IS
STILL AGELESS.

James Broughton

NOTHING SEEMS REAL EXCEPT THE UNREAL.

Oliver Wendell Holmes Sr
on old age

TRUE TERROR IS TO WAKE
UP ONE MORNING AND
DISCOVER THAT YOUR
HIGH SCHOOL CLASS IS
RUNNING THE COUNTRY.

KURT VONNEGUT

YOUTH IS THE TIME FOR ADVENTURES OF THE BODY,

BUT AGE FOR THE TRIUMPHS OF THE MIND.

Logan Pearsall Smith

LIKE MANY WOMEN MY AGE, I AM 28 YEARS OLD.

Mary Schmich

—

AGE DOES NOT
DIMINISH THE EXTREME
DISAPPOINTMENT
OF HAVING A SCOOP
OF ICE CREAM FALL
FROM THE CONE.

—

JIM FIEBIG

INSIDE EVERY OLDER PERSON IS A YOUNGER PERSON

- WONDERING WHAT THE HELL HAPPENED.

Cora Harvey Armstrong

THE SECRET
TO ETERNAL
YOUTH IS
ARRESTED
DEVELOPMENT.

Alice Roosevelt Longworth

WHEN YOU'RE A YOUNG
MAN, MACBETH IS A
CHARACTER PART.
**WHEN YOU'RE OLDER,
IT'S A STRAIGHT PART.**

Laurence Olivier

NOBODY GROWS OLD
MERELY BY LIVING A
NUMBER OF YEARS. WE
GROW OLD BY DESERTING
OUR IDEALS. YEARS MAY
WRINKLE THE SKIN, BUT
TO GIVE UP ENTHUSIASM
WRINKLES THE SOUL.

Samuel Ullman

I HAVE THE BODY
OF AN 18-YEAR-OLD.
I KEEP IT
IN THE FRIDGE.

SPIKE MILLIGAN

THE AGEING PROCESS HAS YOU FIRMLY IN ITS GRASP

IF YOU NEVER GET THE URGE TO THROW A SNOWBALL.

Doug Larson

OLDER AND

WISER?

EVERYTHING I KNOW I LEARNED AFTER I WAS 30.

GEORGES CLEMENCEAU

MINDS RIPEN
AT VERY
DIFFERENT AGES.

Elizabeth Montagu

—

YOU CAN JUDGE YOUR AGE BY THE AMOUNT OF PAIN YOU FEEL WHEN YOU COME IN CONTACT WITH A NEW IDEA.

—

PEARL S. BUCK

THE FIRST SIGN OF
MATURITY IS

THE DISCOVERY THAT THE VOLUME KNOB ALSO TURNS TO THE LEFT.

Jerry M. Wright

TAKE CARE OF THE MINUTES, AND THE HOURS WILL TAKE CARE OF THEMSELVES.

Lord Chesterfield

A MAN IS NOT OLD UNTIL
HIS REGRETS TAKE THE
PLACE OF DREAMS.

John Barrymore

AGE CONSIDERS; YOUTH VENTURES.

Rabindranath Tagore

**AGEING SEEMS
TO BE THE ONLY
AVAILABLE WAY TO
LIVE A LONG LIFE.**

Kitty O'Neill Collins

KNOWLEDGE
SPEAKS,
BUT WISDOM
LISTENS.

Jimi Hendrix

NO ONE OVER 35 IS
WORTH MEETING WHO
HAS NOT SOMETHING
TO TEACH US –
SOMETHING MORE
THAN WE COULD
LEARN BY OURSELVES,
FROM A BOOK.

CYRIL CONNOLLY

YOU'VE HEARD OF THE THREE AGES OF MAN

– YOUTH, AGE,
AND 'YOU
ARE LOOKING
WONDERFUL'.

Francis Spellman

WE HAVE
NO SIMPLE
PROBLEMS
OR EASY DECISIONS
AFTER KINDERGARTEN.

WILLIAM DEAN HOWELLS

—

AS ONE YOUNG
MAN LEAVES HIS
TWENTIES BEHIND,
IDEALISM GIVES WAY
TO PRACTICALITY.
ALMOST.

—

BORUCH LEFF

GOOD JUDGEMENT COMES FROM EXPERIENCE,

AND OFTEN EXPERIENCE COMES FROM BAD JUDGEMENT.

Rita Mae Brown

THE SECRET TO
STAYING YOUNG IS
TO LIVE HONESTLY,
EAT SLOWLY, AND LIE
ABOUT YOUR AGE.

Lucille Ball

WE ARE YOUNG ONLY
ONCE; AFTER THAT
WE NEED SOME
OTHER EXCUSE.

Anonymous

LIVE, LOVE
AND
LAST

NEVER BE AFRAID TO TRY SOMETHING NEW.

Bob Hope

IF I HAD MY LIFE TO LIVE OVER AGAIN,

I WOULD MAKE THE SAME MISTAKES, ONLY SOONER.

Tallulah Bankhead

HE WHO
LAUGHS, LASTS!

Mary Pettibone Poole

I'M NOT AGEING. I JUST
NEED RE-POTTING.

ANONYMOUS

IF I'M
FEELING WILD,

I DON'T FLOSS BEFORE BEDTIME.

Judith Viorst

—

THE PROBLEM WITH THE WORLD IS THAT EVERYONE IS A FEW DRINKS BEHIND.

—

HUMPHREY BOGART

AS MEN GET OLDER, THE TOYS GET MORE EXPENSIVE.

Marvin Davis

YOU ARE ONLY
YOUNG ONCE,
BUT YOU CAN
BE IMMATURE
FOR A LIFETIME.

John P. Grier

THE KEY TO SUCCESSFUL
AGEING IS TO PAY
**AS LITTLE ATTENTION
TO IT AS POSSIBLE.**

Judith Regan

SEIZE THE MOMENT.
REMEMBER ALL
THOSE WOMEN ON
THE *TITANIC*

WHO WAVED OFF THE
DESSERT CART.

Erma Bombeck

**EVERYTHING
SLOWS DOWN WITH AGE,
EXCEPT THE TIME
IT TAKES CAKE AND
ICE CREAM TO
REACH YOUR HIPS.**

John Wagner

ILLS, PILLS AND TWINGES

THEY SAY THAT
AGE IS ALL IN
YOUR MIND.

**THE TRICK
IS KEEPING
IT FROM
CREEPING
DOWN INTO
YOUR BODY.**

Anonymous

LIFE WOULD BE
INFINITELY HAPPIER
IF WE COULD ONLY
BE BORN AT THE AGE
OF 80 AND GRADUALLY
APPROACH 18.

MARK TWAIN

AS FOR ME,
EXCEPT FOR AN
OCCASIONAL
HEART ATTACK,
I FEEL AS YOUNG
AS I EVER DID.

ROBERT BENCHLEY

—

I KEEP FIT. EVERY
MORNING I DO A
HUNDRED LAPS OF
AN OLYMPIC-SIZED
SWIMMING POOL
IN A SMALL
MOTOR LAUNCH.

—

PETER COOK

MEN, LIKE PEACHES AND
PEARS, GROW SWEET A
LITTLE WHILE BEFORE
THEY BEGIN TO DECAY.

Oliver Wendell Holmes Sr

YOU'RE NOT OLD
UNTIL IT TAKES YOU
LONGER TO REST UP
**THAN IT DOES
TO GET TIRED.**

Forrest Clare 'Phog' Allen

IF YOU REST,
YOU RUST.

Helen Hayes

I DON'T DO
ALCOHOL ANY MORE

- I GET THE SAME EFFECT JUST STANDING UP FAST.

Anonymous

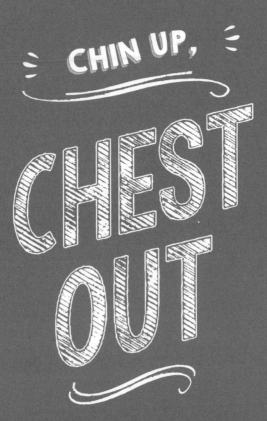

CHIN UP, CHEST OUT

**AFTER 30,
A BODY HAS A
MIND OF ITS OWN.**

Bette Midler

CHEERFULNESS AND CONTENT ARE GREAT BEAUTIFIERS,

AND ARE FAMOUS PRESERVERS OF YOUTHFUL LOOKS.

Charles Dickens

TIME MAY BE A GREAT HEALER, BUT IT'S A LOUSY BEAUTICIAN.

Anonymous

HOW PLEASANT IS THE
DAY WHEN WE GIVE UP
STRIVING TO BE YOUNG
OR SLENDER.

WILLIAM JAMES

WRINKLES
ARE HEREDITARY.

PARENTS GET
THEM FROM
THEIR CHILDREN.

Doris Day

—

AS YOU AGE NATURALLY,
YOUR FAMILY SHOWS
MORE AND MORE ON
YOUR FACE. IF YOU
DENY THAT, YOU DENY
YOUR HERITAGE.

—

FRANCES CONROY

ALAS, AFTER
A CERTAIN AGE
EVERY MAN IS
RESPONSIBLE FOR
HIS FACE.

Albert Camus

ONE DAY YOU LOOK
IN THE MIRROR AND
REALISE THE FACE
**YOU ARE SHAVING IS
YOUR FATHER'S.**

Robert Harris

AS WE GROW OLD, THE BEAUTY STEALS INWARD.

RALPH WALDO EMERSON

AGE IS WHATEVER YOU THINK IT IS.

YOU ARE AS OLD AS YOU THINK YOU ARE.

Muhammad Ali

If you're interested in finding out more
about our books, find us on Facebook
at **Summersdale Publishers**
and follow us on Twitter at
@Summersdale.

www.summersdale.com